STAND UP  SPEAK OUT

ENVIRONMENTAL RIGHTS

Virginia Loh-Hagan

1

45° 45TH PARALLEL PRESS

Published in the United States of America by Cherry Lake Publishing Group
Ann Arbor, Michigan
www.cherrylakepublishing.com

Reading Adviser: Beth Walker Gambro, MS, Ed., Reading Consultant, Yorkville, IL
Book Designer: Jen Wahi

Photo Credits: © Sheila Fitzgerald/Shutterstock.com, 4; © Valmedia/Shutterstock.com, 6; © Beau van den Buuse/
Shutterstock.com, 8; © nicostock/Shutterstock.com, 11; © YAKOBCHUK VIACHESLAV/Shutterstock.com, 12; © Vladimir
Melnikov/Shutterstock.com, 14; © Dmitry Rukhlenko/Shutterstock.com, 17; © Rich Carey/Shutterstock.com, 18; © Andrii
Zastrozhnov/Shutterstock.com, 20; © triocean/Shutterstock.com, 23; © vchal/Shutterstock.com, 24; © Diego G Diaz/
Shutterstock.com, 26; © Andrew Stripes/Shutterstock.com, 29; © SewCream/Shutterstock.com, 30, additional cover
images courtesy of iStock.com

45th Parallel Press is an imprint of Cherry Lake Publishing Group.

Library of Congress Cataloging-in-Publication Data

Names: Loh-Hagan, Virginia, author.
Title: Environmental rights / by Virginia Loh-Hagan.
Description: Ann Arbor, Michigan : Cherry Lake Publishing, [2021] | Series:
   Stand up, speak out | Includes bibliographical references and index.
Identifiers: LCCN 2021004957 (print) | LCCN 2021004958 (ebook) | ISBN
   9781534187511 (hardcover) | ISBN 9781534188914 (paperback) | ISBN
   9781534190313 (pdf) | ISBN 9781534191716 (ebook)
Subjects: LCSH: Environmentalism–Juvenile literature.
Classification: LCC GE195.5 .L64 2021 (print) | LCC GE195.5 (ebook) | DDC
   333.72–dc23
LC record available at https://lccn.loc.gov/2021004957
LC ebook record available at https://lccn.loc.gov/2021004958

Printed in the United States of America
Corporate Graphics

About the Author:

Dr. Virginia Loh-Hagan is an author, university professor, and former classroom teacher. She's currently the Director of the Asian Pacific Islander Desi American Resource Center at San Diego State University. She practices recycling and upcycling. She lives in San Diego with her very tall husband and very naughty dogs.

TABLE OF CONTENTS

TAKE POLLUTION DOWN TO

OUR generation OUR CHOICE

YOUTH

DENIAL IS NOT A POLICY

● Activists often work as a group.
They have power in numbers.

WHAT IS ENVIRONMENTAL ACTIVISM?

Everyone has the power to make our world a better place. A person just has to act. **Activists** fight for change. They fight for their beliefs. They see unfair things. They want to correct wrongs. They want **justice**. Justice is upholding what is right. Activists help others. They serve people and communities.

There are many problems in the world. Activists seek to solve these problems. They learn all they can. They raise awareness. They take action. They inspire others to act.

Activists care very deeply about their **causes**. Causes are principles, aims, or movements. They give rise to activism.

Many activists feel strongly about the **environment**. The environment is everything around us. It includes living and nonliving things. It includes the air, land, and oceans.

Many environment activists believe humans are **exploiting** the Earth. Exploit means to use in a selfish way. Activists want to save the planet. They want to protect natural resources. They support being green. This means keeping our world clean. It means being **sustainable**. Sustainable means using resources in a way that we could keep doing for a long time.

In this book, we share examples of environmental issues and actions. We also share tips for how to engage. Your activist journey starts here!

● Being green also means being eco-friendly.

GET STARTED

Community service is about helping others. It's about creating a kinder world. Activism goes beyond service. It's about making a fairer and more just world. It involves acting and fighting for change. Choose to be an activist!

○ **Focus on your cause!** In addition to the topics covered in this book, there are many others. Other examples include saving natural habitats and living in a more sustainable way.

○ **Do your research!** Learn all you can about the cause. Learn about the history. Learn from other activists.

○ **Make a plan!** Get organized.

○ **Make it happen!** Act! There are many ways to act. Activists write letters. They write petitions. They protest. They march in the streets. They ban or **boycott**. Boycott means to avoid or not buy something as a protest. They perform art to make people aware. They post to social media. They fight to change laws. They organize sit-in events. They participate in demonstrations and **strikes**. During strikes, people protest by refusing to do something, such as work.

● Methane gas released from cows is one of the biggest contributors to global warming.

CHAPTER 1

ADDRESS CLIMATE CHANGE

Climate refers to the weather in an area. Climate change is when the weather changes too much over time. It's a change in temperature and rainfall. Earth's overall climate is changing too quickly. It's becoming warmer. This causes many issues. Sea levels are rising. Mountain icebergs are getting smaller. There are more storms, heat waves, and dry periods.

Climate change is caused by human activities. Activities include things like burning fuel, increasing cow farming, and driving cars. Such activities cause gases to get trapped in Earth's atmosphere. These gases block heat from escaping. This warms up Earth.

GET INSPIRED

BY PIONEERS IN ENVIRONMENTAL RIGHTS ACTIVISM!

○ **John Muir** was called "John of the Mountains." He founded the national parks system. He fought to preserve Yosemite National Park in California. In 1892, he founded the Sierra Club. The club started as a club for mountain lovers. Today, it protects U.S. natural areas.

○ **Aldo Leopold** was a professor of wildlife management. He believed in creating a caring relationship between people and nature. He viewed nature as "a community to which we belong." His ideas inspire many environmental activists today. He promoted the wise use of land and water resources. In 1924, he developed the first national wilderness area in the United States.

○ **Wangari Maathai** was a Kenyan activist. She was the first African woman to win the Nobel Peace Prize. She was the first East and Central African woman to get a doctorate degree. In 1977, she founded the Green Belt movement. She helped women plant more than 20 million trees.

● Climate change is also known as global warming.

Greta Thunberg is famous for being a teen climate change activist. She inspired a youth climate movement. She hosted strikes in front of the Swedish government building. She protested by skipping school. She sat in front of government buildings. Today, Greta meets with world leaders. She makes speeches. In 2019, she led the Global Week for Future. This was the largest climate change strike in world history. It was a series of international strikes. People demanded action to address climate change.

Consider a green career. These are jobs that work to solve climate change.

Leonardo DiCaprio is a famous actor. He works with many environmental activist groups. He funds many projects. He uses his star power to address climate change. He made a film showing the effects of climate change. He makes people more aware of the issues.

Stand Up, Speak Out

Each of us has a **carbon footprint**. This is the amount of gases released into the air because of your actions. Activists want us to reduce our carbon footprints. You can help!

> Challenge your family and friends to go "car-free." Driving adds gases to the air. Instead of driving, bike or walk. If people have to drive, they can **carpool**. Carpool means to share rides.

> Encourage your family and school to **upcycle**. Upcycle means to reuse things. Making new products adds gases. Upcycling helps people buy less. Organize bins to collect things. Host parties to turn old things into new things. Get creative.

● Forests cover 30 percent of Earth's land.

CHAPTER 2

END DEFORESTATION

Deforestation is the clearing or cutting down of forests. Humans use wood to make things such as furniture. They clear land of trees to build on or to use for farming.

Trees help keep the planet safe. They make oxygen, which helps us breathe. They absorb gases from the air. When humans cut down trees, we lose a layer of protection. The gases stored in trees are released into the air. This leads to climate change.

Deforestation also kills plants and animals. Animals and people living in these forests lose their homes. Deforestation also causes land **erosion**. Erosion means the process of wearing away. Trees hold soil together. Without soil, the land can slide or blow away.

GET INSPIRED

BY LEGAL VICTORIES

○ Rachel Carson wrote *Silent Spring* in 1962. She wrote about the dangers of chemical pesticides. Her book led to a ban of pesticides. In 1969, 2 environmental disasters happened in the United States. One was an oil spill off the coast of Santa Barbara, California. The other was a river in Ohio that caught on fire because of oil **pollution**. Pollution is the introduction of harmful materials into the environment. These events made people worry about human impacts on the environment. They wanted a national environmental policy. Carson's book and the disasters inspired several bills and policies. They led to the creation of the U.S. Environmental Protection Agency (EPA) in 1970.

○ Native people living in the Amazon rainforest in Ecuador had their land taken over by oil companies. The people fought for a new constitution. In 2008, Ecuador recognized the rights of nature in its constitution. It was the first country to do so. It didn't see nature as property. It gave Native people the right to protect and restore the environment.

Rainforests are in tropical areas. They're the largest areas being cut down. Paul Pavol fights to save Papua New Guinea's rainforests. He fights against the logging companies. He sets up roadblocks. He stops trucks from moving the logs.

Rudi Putra works to protect Indonesian rainforests. He wants to save rhinos that live in the rainforests.

● Experts think rainforests will disappear within 100 years.

He pushes the government to enforce laws to protect nature. He organized a worldwide petition. More than 1.4 million people signed it. Putra brought a lot of attention to his cause. He organizes more than 150 guards to patrol the area. These guards destroy traps. They stop hunters. They stop illegal loggers. They help protect the rainforests.

● We lose about 36 football fields of forests every minute.

Stand Up, Speak Out

Paper products are made from trees. These products include toilet paper, boxes, tissues, and more. Humans use a lot of paper. This means more trees need to be cut down. Activists want to save forests. You can help!

➤ Start a **campaign** to save paper. Campaigns are courses of action. Encourage people to recycle or reuse paper. Show people how they can go digital. Going digital means to do more online.

➤ Write emails to companies sending **junk mail**. Junk mail is ads sent in the mail. Ask companies to stop making and sending paper ads. Also, mailing requires mail carriers to travel. Stopping junk mail would save paper and gas.

Turtles mistake floating plastic bags for food. The bags look like jellyfish.

CHAPTER 3

REDUCE PLASTIC TRASH

Humans use a lot of plastic products. Single-use plastic is a problem. These are plastic products we use once and throw away. Single-use plastic makes up more than 40 percent of plastic trash. It includes bags, drink bottles, straws, and wrappers. Tons of plastic ends up in the ocean. Plastic doesn't **decompose** back into nature. Decompose means to break down. Plastic trash stays in the ocean or **landfills** forever. Landfills are places that store trash. They release gases into the air.

Plastic trash is killing sea turtles. An activist group made a video. The video showed scientists pulling a plastic straw out of a sea turtle's nose. This video went viral. It increased awareness of the issue.

GET IN THE KNOW

KNOW THE HISTORY

○ **1306** King Edward I ruled England. He banned coal burning in London. The coal caused a lot of smoke. Anyone who sold and burned coal could have been tortured or killed.

○ **1730** Amrita Devi Bishnoi was an early activist in India. A king wanted to build a new palace. He sent soldiers to get trees from a forest in the village of Khejarli. The villagers fought the king's soldiers. Bishnoi hugged the trees. She encouraged others to do the same. She was killed along with the other tree-huggers. Their sacrifice is still remembered today. It inspired later environmental movements.

○ **1974** President Gerald Ford signed the Safe Drinking Water Act. This was the first law that oversaw U.S. drinking water. It makes sure that tap water is safe.

○ **2006** Vice President Al Gore narrated a film called *An Inconvenient Truth*. He shared the dangers of global warming. This film raised awareness about climate change. He was awarded a Nobel Peace Prize.

● Before the ban, California used more than 13 billion single-use plastic bags every year.

Californians Against Waste is an environmental activist group. They fight for stronger environmental laws. They fight for more recycling programs. In 2014, they worked with politicians. They campaigned for votes. In 2016, California became the first state to ban single-use plastic bags. This inspired other states to do the same.

GreenHub is an environmental activist group in Vietnam. It was founded by 3 Vietnamese women. Vietnam is one of the top 5 countries causing plastic pollution. GreenHub members track sources of plastic trash. They teach communities about the bad effects of plastic trash. They show people how to reduce plastic trash.

● The average American sends nearly 5 pounds (2.3 kilograms) of trash to the landfill every day.

Stand Up, Speak Out

Some people are zero-waste activists. They send nothing to the landfill. They reduce what they buy. They reuse or recycle what they can. Activists want to reduce waste. You can help!

> Don't waste any food scraps. Learn to make **compost** and teach others to do it. Compost is decayed plants and food materials. It's used to improve soil.

> Start a campaign against plastic straws. Straws are thrown away. They create waste. Encourage people to use paper or metal straws.

> Host workshops. Teach others how to make their own products. Buy fewer things from stores.

About 1 million people die each year from water or sewage-related sicknesses.

CHAPTER 4

FIGHT FOR CLEAN WATER

Environmental activism is about making sure all humans have equal access to natural resources. It pushes more developed countries to not waste resources. It wants less developed communities to have the same access to resources. Humans need access to safe water and **sewage** systems. Sewage is human waste. Sewage systems get rid of poisons in water. They stop the spread of sicknesses. They keep germs out of the environment.

Poor communities may not have clean water. They may not have good sewage systems. Georgie Badiel is a model from West Africa. As a young girl, she spent 3 hours getting water. She co-wrote a children's book about clean water access. She also builds wells for her hometown.

GET INVOLVED

Several groups work to protect the environment. Connect with them to get more involved.

- **The Environmental Defense Fund (EDF)** finds solutions to environmental problems. It focuses on climate change, oceans, and air pollution. It bases their actions on science.

- **Greening Forward** was founded by a 12-year-old. It's the largest youth-led group in the U.S. It provides grants and plants trees. It leads recycling campaigns to reduce landfill waste.

- **The Student Conservation Association (SCA)** wants to protect nature. The SCA protects and restores national parks and other community green spaces.

- **The Waterkeeper Alliance** fights for clean water. It wants every community to have drinkable, fishable, and swimmable water. It tracks down polluters. It fights for laws. It provides training.

- **Zero Hour** is a youth-led movement. The youth leaders are focused on acting on climate change. They provide training and resources. They host meetings and marches.

BE kind to every kind

Matt Damon is a famous actor. He founded Water.org. This group helped more than 33 million people get access to safe water and sewage systems.

Casi Callaway is from Mobile, Alabama. In 1999, she discovered human waste spilling into the bay. She filed Mobile's first lawsuit for Clean Water Act violations. She fought to stop more spills.

● Consider using reusable water bottles instead of plastic ones.

Mari Copeny is from Flint, Michigan. In 2016, at age 8, she wrote a letter to President Barack Obama about her city's water. Flint's water has poisonous metals. Obama went to Flint. He helped the city get money to start fixing the problem. Mari uses Twitter to educate others. She started a Dear Flint Kids project. The goal is to send Flint kids positive messages.

Some water activists fight to **conserve** water. Conserve means to save.

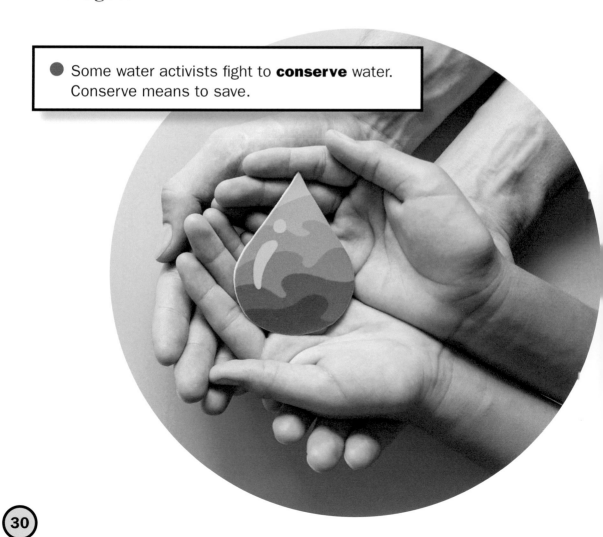

Stand Up, Speak Out

In less developed countries, women and girls are responsible for getting water. They must walk several hours to get water each day. This means they can't do anything else. They can't go to school. They can't take care of their families. Activists want to help communities get safe water. You can help!

> Ask people to donate to clean water activist groups. Host events to raise money.

> Host a water walk. Show people how others without easy access to water live. Have people hold water jugs. Have them walk for an hour. Talk about the experience.

> Celebrate World Water Day on March 22. Talk about the importance of water. Make posters.

GLOSSARY

activists (AK-tih-vists) people who fight for political or social change

boycott (BOI-kot) to refuse to buy something or take part in something as a protest to force change

campaign (kam-PAYN) an organized course of action

carbon footprint (KAR-buhn FUT-print) an amount of greenhouse gases released into the air because of one's actions

carpool (KAR-pool) traveling in one car, with each person taking turns driving

causes (KAWZ-es) the reasons for activism

climate (KLYE-mit) the weather of an area over time

compost (KOM-post) decayed organic material used to fertilize soil

conserve (kuhn-SERVE) to save

decompose (dee-kuhm-POZE) to break down and return to nature

deforestation (di-for-uh-STAY-shuhn) the process of the clearing or cutting down of forests

environment (en-VYE-ruhn-muhnt) living and nonliving things around us like air, land, and oceans

erosion (i-ROH-zhuhn) the process of wearing away

exploiting (ek-SPLOYT-ing) using in a selfish way

junk mail (JUHNGK MAYL) ads or promotions sent via mail or email

justice (JUHSS-tiss) the upholding of what is fair and right

landfills (LAND-fils) areas of land used to store trash

pollution (puh-LOO-shuhn) the introduction of harmful materials into the environment

sewage (SOO-ij) human waste

strikes (STRYKES) organized protests where people refuse to do something

sustainable (suh-STAY-nuh-buhl) using resources in a way that allows us to continue to do so for a long time

upcycle (UHP-sye-kuhl) to reuse things or to make something old into something new

LEARN MORE!

French, Jess. *What A Waste: Trash, Recycling, and Protecting Our Planet.* New York, NY: DK Children, 2019.

Herman, Gail. *What Is Climate Change?* New York, NY: Penguin Workshop, 2018.

McDaniel, Melissa. *Facing a Warming World: Understanding Climate Change.* New York, NY: Children's Press, 2020.

Van Frankenhuyzen, Robbyn Smith, and Eileen Ryan Ewen (illust.). *H is for Honeybee: A Beekeeping Alphabet.* Ann Arbor, MI: Sleeping Bear Press, 2020.

INDEX